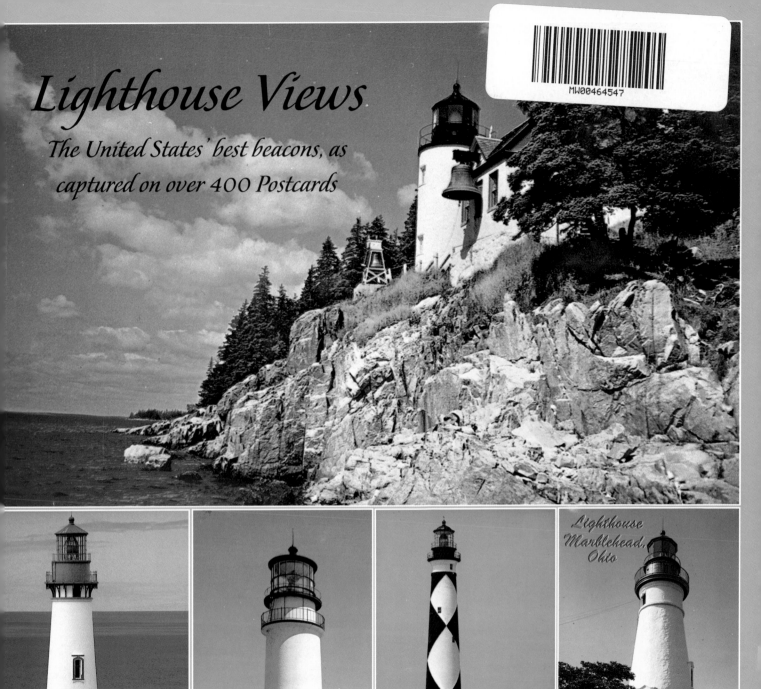

Lighthouse Views

The United States' best beacons, as captured on over 400 Postcards

Mary L. Martin
with Tina Skinner

Schiffer Publishing Ltd

4880 Lower Valley Road, Atglen, PA 19310 USA

BOYS & GIRLS CLUBS
OF HARFORD COUNTY

The Boys & Girls Clubs of Harford County is grateful to Mary Martin Postcards for naming it a beneficiary of royalty proceeds from this wonderful book on lighthouses.

The Boys and Girls Club of Harford County, Maryland, is a nonprofit youth development agency that serves more than 3,000 children and youth ages 6-18 annually. The club's mission is to inspire and enable all young people, especially those from disadvantaged circumstances, to realize their full potential as productive, responsible, and caring citizens. The program offers researched-based programs in character and leadership development, education, career development, health and life skills, the arts, sports, fitness, and recreation. All staff is screened and background-checked. The club is an affiliate of Boys & Girls Clubs of America, a 150-year-old movement to provide opportunities for young people.

Library of Congress Cataloging-in-Publication Data:

Martin, Mary L., 1936-
  Lighthouse views : the United States best beacons, as captured on over 400 postcards / by Mary L. Martin with Tina Skinner.
       p. cm.
  ISBN 0-7643-2087-4 (pbk.)
1. Lighthouses—United States—Pictorial works. 2. Lighthouses in art. I. Skinner, Tina. II. Title.
VK1023.M37 2004
387.1'55'0973—dc22

2004009111

Designed by John P. Cheek
Type set in Florens LP/Humanist 521 Lt BT
ISBN: 0-7643-2087-4
Printed in China
1 2 3 4

Published by Schiffer Publishing Ltd.
4880 Lower Valley Road
Atglen, PA 19310
Phone: (610) 593-1777; Fax: (610) 593-2002
E-mail: Info@schifferbooks.com

For the largest selection of fine reference books on this and related subjects, please visit our web site at
www.schifferbooks.com
We are always looking for people to write books on new and related subjects. If you have an idea for a book please contact us at the above address.

This book may be purchased from the publisher.
Include $3.95 for shipping.
Please try your bookstore first.
You may write for a free catalog.

In Europe, Schiffer books are distributed by
Bushwood Books
6 Marksbury Ave.
Kew Gardens
Surrey TW9 4JF England
Phone: 44 (0) 20 8392-8585; Fax: 44 (0) 20 8392-9876
E-mail: info@bushwoodbooks.co.uk
Free postage in the U.K., Europe; air mail at cost.

Contents

Introduction

There's a whole cast of lighthouse aficionados living in the world. No doubt you're one of them, in that you have bought and are enjoying this book. If you are new to this world, welcome to the club. Lighthouse lovers fill their lawns with lighthouse statues, their windows with lighthouse figurines. Their fantasies focus on lives spent watching a rocky shoreline, far from neighbors and yet a lifeline to seafaring folk in need of guidance.

This subset of people spend their annual allowance of vacation days in hot pursuit of lighthouses. They choose a shoreline, stock up on maps, and set out to visit and photograph every publicly accessed lighthouse. They may charter a private boat to help them view more remote towers, or a small plane or helicopter in extreme cases. They time their vacations to coincide with the often brief open seasons when tours of lighthouse interiors are available. They count every step, study every facet of a Fresnel lens, and steep themselves in the history of these important beacons. Just as lighthouses serve as beacons to sailors, they also beckon tourists!

In the world of postcard collecting, people follow their heart. They may collect their hometown, or a summer resort they enjoyed in their childhood. They may collect a favorite animal, flower, or floral artist. High among the all-time favorite postcard collecting themes are lighthouses. This is hardly news. We found postcards dating back to the turn of the century (the 20th Century) inscribed and sent to a friend "for your lighthouse collection."

Just as the towers lure avid viewers, postcard collectors seek the innumerable postcards they have been featured upon. Thousands of postcards have been published on lighthouses around the world since the turn of the century. The popularity of these images continued on through the linen era and into today's chrome period. Few beach resorts can be found that don't offer tourists views of the nearest lighthouse ready to post off to friends.

Lighthouse postcard collectors enjoy a wonderful opportunity to witness the transformations wrought over time on these historic structures, making their hobby more interesting and rewarding. Because so many lighthouses have been valiantly fought for and lovingly restored and preserved, they are landmarks that are still high on sightseeing lists, and still avidly captured for postcard images.

If you are in want of other avid lighthouse fans for friends, or simply more information about lighthouse postcards you have collected, a good place to start is the United States Lighthouse Society. The Society has over 6,000 members who collect artifacts and lore about lighthouses and light ships. It publishes a quarterly magazine and offers educational material to schools. The society can be contacted at 244 Kearny St., 5th floor, San Francisco, CA 94108; 415-362-7255.

We the authors wish you the best of luck in your pursuit of the perfect view, be it up close and in person, or on a historic postcard.

Valuing Postcards

The values shown in this book are provided as a guideline for collectors and dealers. The values are based upon rarity of the postcard views. Condition has not been factored in and should be considered when evaluating individual postcards.

A Short History of the Postcard in the United States

Pioneer Era (1893-1898)

Although there were earlier scattered issues, most pioneer cards in today's collections begin with the cards placed on sale at the Columbian Exposition in Chicago, Illinois, on May 1, 1893. These were illustrations on government printed postal cards and privately printed souvenir cards. The government postal cards had the printed one-cent stamp, while the souvenir cards required a two-cent adhesive postage stamp to be applied. Writing was not permitted on the address side of the cards.

Private Mailing Card Era (1898-1901)

On May 19, 1898, private printers were granted permission, by an act of Congress, to print and sell cards that bore the inscription "Private Mailing Card." Today, we call these cards "PMCs." Postage required was now a one-cent adhesive stamp. A dozen or more American printers began to take postcards seriously. Writing was still not permitted on the address side.

Postcard Era (1901-1907)

The use of the word "Postcard" was granted by the government to private printers on December 24, 1901. Writing was still not permitted on the address side. In this era, private citizens began to take black-and-white photographs and have them printed on paper with postcard backs.

Divided Back Era (1907-1914)

Postcards with a divided back were permitted March 1, 1907. The address was to be written on the right side and the left side was for writing messages. Many millions of cards were published and printed in this era, most in Germany, where printers were far more advanced in the lithographic processes. With the advent of World War I, the supply of postcards had to come from England and the United States.

White Border Era (1915-1930)

Most domestic-use postcards were printed in the United States during this period. To save ink, a border was left around the view, thus the name "White Border Cards." The high cost of labor, inexperience, and public taste created cards of inferior quality. Competition in a narrowing market caused many publishers to go out of business.

Linen Era (1930-1944)

New printing processes allowed printing on postcards with high rag content that caused a linen-like finish. These cheap cards allowed for the use of gaudy dyes for coloring. Curt Teich's line of linen postcards flourished. Many important historical events are recorded on these cards.

Photochrome Era (1945 to present)

The chrome postcards started to dominate the scene soon after they were launched by the Union Oil Company in their western service stations in 1939. Mike Roberts pioneered with his "WESCO" cards soon after World War II. Three-dimensional postcards also appeared during this era.

excerpted from **The Lighthouse**

The rocky ledge runs far into the sea,
and on its outer point, some miles away,
the lighthouse lifts its massive masonry,
A pillar of fire by night, of cloud by day…

And as the evening darkens, lo! how bright,
through the deep purple of the twilight air,
Beams forth the sudden radiance of its light
with strange, unearthly splendor in the glare!

No one alone; from each projecting cape
And perilous reef along the ocean's verge,
Starts into life a dim, gigantic shape,
Holding its lantern o'er the restless surge…

Steadfast, serene, immovable, the same
Year after year, through all the silent night
Burns on forevermore that quenchless flame,
Shines on that inextinguishable light!

by Henry Wadsworth Longfellow

Lighthouse Views

Alaska

c. 1980s, Michael Anderson Photo, Greatland Classic Sales Co., Inc. [$4-6]

Eldred Rock Lighthouse, located in the Lynn Canal.

© 1997 Michael W. Siegrist Sr., Outdoor Photo [$4-6]

Northhead Lighthouse was built on a bluff near Cape Disappointment, at the mouth of the Columbia River, in 1898. Before jetties were built, this was one of the most treacherous river bars in the world. More than 230 ships were wrecked here.

Rockwell Lighthouse overlooking Sitka Sound.

California

Battery Point Lighthouse, Crescent City, CA. Built in 1856 on a small island approximately 200 yards from shore, it is accessible at low tide.

Fort Point Lighthouse, San Francisco. Marking the entrance to the harbor, the light has had a checkered history of being built (first in 1853), torn down, and rebuilt as changes were made to the fort that occupied the same site. The current structure was deactivated in 1934, and is closed to the public because of the hazardous lead paint chips that have rained on it from the Golden Gate Bridge above.

1751-Pigeon Point Light House, Coast of California

Pigeon Point Lighthouse, Pescadero. Established in 1871, the 115-foot tower marks the southern approach to the San Francisco Bay.

Point Arena Lighthouse. Originally built in 1856, then rebuilt after the great 1906 earthquake, the 115-foot tower doubles as a perfect perch for whale watching.

Point Bonita Lighthouse, Marin Headlands. Guarding the entrance to the San Francisco Bay, in 1854 this scenic vantage became home to the first Pacific Coast lighthouse and fog signal. Still isolated, it is reached via a long walk from the parking area, through a tunnel and across the lighthouse system's only suspension bridge.

Point Cabrillo Light Station, Mendocino. Built in 1908 to protect the coastal trade in lumber from the North coast to San Francisco.

18:—OLD SPANISH LIGHT HOUSE, POINT LOMA, CALIF.

1931, M. Kashower Co., Los Angeles [$5-7]

c. 1970s, F.D. Schmidt Photo, Western Publ. & Nov. Co., Los Angeles [$4-6]

Cabrillo National Monument, Point Loma. Put into service in 1855, the popular tourist attraction came to be known as the Old Spanish Light House. After restoration, it became the most visited monument in America. Many, many postcards have been produced over the years, from those showing the site in ruins, to current day cards that celebrate the carefully restored structure.

c. 1970s, Mitock & Sons, 7410 Greenbush Ave., North Hollywood, CA [$4-6]

The Lighthouse at Fisherman's Village, Marina Del Rey, was built to replicate early New England towers. Visitors are treated to a view of up to 50 miles.

c. 1940s, Stanley A. Piltz Co., San Francisco [$5-7]

Mile Rock Lighthouse, Lands End, stood guard to the San Francisco Bay before the Golden Gate Bridge was built.

Point Fermin Light, San Pedro Harbor, Los Angeles. Constructed in 1874, the tower and dwelling were both designed in the Italianate style. The light was deactivated in 1942, when many lights were deactivated because of WWII.

c. 1910, Souvenir Publishing Co., Los Angeles & S.F. [$6-8]

Point Loma Lighthouse, San Diego. This new steel tower that replaced the "Old Spanish Lighthouse" in 1891 continues as a guide to navigation and an active Coast Guard station.

1908, E.P. Charlton & Co., San Diego [$5-7]

Port Pinos Lighthouse, Pacific Grove. The West Coast's oldest operating lighthouse, it has been guiding ships to the southern entrance of Monterey Bay since 1855. It is now fenced off and surrounded by a golf course.

c. 1990s, Ken Glaser, Jr. Photo, Smith Novelty Co., San Francisco [$4-6]

c. 1970s, Randy Larson Photo, Bell Magazine Agency, Monterey, CA [$4-6]

Point Sur Lighthouse, Monterey. Built in 1889, this Romanesque-style sandstone building was constructed on bar rock. A restoration of the site – which includes all of its 19th century light station buildings intact (blacksmith/carpenter shop, radio beacon, pump house, barracks, barn, cistern, oil house, garage, wood/sandstone assistant keeper's dwelling, and original marine railways) – is underway.

Point Reyes Lighthouse, Gulf of the Farallones. The Lighthouse Board realized the importance of a beacon here, in one of the foggiest places in North America, back in 1855. However, winds, remote location, and rocky terrain helped delay completion until 1870.

c. 1960s, Marin Color Cards, Inverness, CA [$4-6]

©1992 Inga Spence Photo/ Western Photo Illuminations, Carson City, NV [$4-6]

St. George Reef Lighthouse, 6 miles west of Point St. George, Crescent City. After eleven years of construction, the lighthouse began operation on October 20, 1892. It was decommissioned in 1975.

Point Vicente Lighthouse, Los Angeles. The 67-foot tower was built in 1926, and continues to operate today as part of a Coast Guard station.

POINT VINCENTE LIGHTHOUSE

c. 1990s, James Blank Photo/ Historic America Series [$4-6]

Santa Cruz Light, Monterey Bay. First lit in 1869, it had to be moved inland 300 feet in 1878 to escape erosion. In 1941 it was decommissioned, and an automated light was placed nearby. The old structure was razed in 1948. In 1965, 18-year-old Mark Abbott drowned while surfing near the point. His parents used the insurance money to build a brick lighthouse near the site of the old light. Completed in 1967, it now houses a surfing museum.

c. 1970s, Pacific Distributors, Pacific Grove, CA [$4-6]

Trinidad Head Lighthouse, Trinidad. This squat, 25-foot tower was first lit in 1871 and continues to aid navigation in Trinidad Harbor.

c. 1975, John F. McNamara Photo/ Columbia View Cards [$4-6]

Yerba Buena (Goat Island) Light, San Francisco. First lit in 1875, the light and Coast Guard Station continue to operate today.

Light House on Yerba Buena Island, San Francisco, Cal.

1915, Pacific Novelty Co., San Francisco [$5-7]

East Island Lighthouse, Lake
Pocotopaug, East Hampton.

c. 1900 [$6-9]

c. 1900, The Bridgeport News Company, CT [$6-9]

Bridgeport Harbor Light House, Bridgeport.

pre-1920, The Hunter Photo Co., Madison, CT [$6-8]

Faulkner Island Light,
Guilford.

1910, C. C. Markham, Guilford, CT [$8-10]

Great Captain Island Light in the northerly side of the westerly part of Long Island Sound.

c. 1910, Hugh C. Leighton Co., Portland, ME [$6-8]

Cornfield Lightship, Old Saybrook.

c. 1910s, James Pharmacy, Old Saybrook, [$8-10]

Green's Reef Light, Norwalk Harbor.

c. 1920s, Elm City Post Card Co., New Haven, CT [$5-7]

Light House Point, New Haven.

c. 1900, S. Langsdorf & Co., N.Y. [$6-8]

c. 1960s, The New London News Co., CT [$4-6]

Greetings From... **The Connecticut Shoreline**

Lynde Point Light, Old Saybrook. Originally known as Inner Light, it is located in Fenwick at the mouth of the Connecticut River on Long Island Sound. Established in 1802.

c. 1990s, Kathleen E. Briggs Photo/ © Book & Tackle, Westerly, RI [$4-6]

The Outer Lighthouse, Old Saybrook, Conn.

Outer Light, Old Saybrook.

c. 1910 [$6-8]

Old Tower Light, New Haven, CT. Constructed in 1840 at a cost of $10,000.

"OLD TOWER LIGHT." LIGHTHOUSE POINT PARK. NEW HAVEN. CONN.

12

61785

NEW LONDON LIGHT HOUSE.

Be sure to see "Ben Hur" at the Worcester. I have given the new P. L. a silver cup. DWS Apr. 23, '04.

LIGHT HOUSE, NEW LONDON, CONN.

New London Harbor Light.

New London Harbor Light. It was built in 1801 on the rocky shore of the Thames River and automated in 1912.

c. 1960s, Tichnor Bros., Inc., Boston, MA [$4-6]

Mystic Seaport Lighthouse, Mystic Seaport. A reproduction of Nantucket's Brant Point Light.

c. 1990s, Bernard Ludwig Gordon Photo/© Book & Tackle Shop, Westerly, RI [$4-6]

Light House. Noank, Conn.

Morgan Point Lighthouse, Noank.

1906, The Rhode Island News Company, Providence, RI [$6-8]

Peck's Ledge Light, South Norwalk, Conn.

25802   © BY G.S. NORTH

Peck's Ledge Light, South Norwalk.

BREAKWATER LIGHT HOUSE BY MOONLIGHT, NEW HAVEN, CONN.

653

Southwest Ledge Lighthouse, New Haven. Once known as Breakwater Lighthouse.

OLD LIGHT HOUSE, NEW HAVEN HARBOR.   601

Just a little reminder of Feb. 10th 1907. Helen - Katherine - Anybody else? well probably not!

Five Mile Point Light, New Haven.

c. 1906, Americ. Hist. Art. Publ. Co., NY [$6-8]

Sperry Light & Breakwater, New Haven.

pre-1920, The Rhode Island News Co., Providence, RI [$6-8]

New London Ledge Light, New London, was known as South West Ledge Light when it was built in 1909.
The name was changed to avoid confusion with New Haven's Southwest Ledge Light.

Stonington Light, West Breakwater, Stonington, Conn.

pre-1920, J. Solomon, New London, CT [$6-8]

Stonington West Breakwater Light, Stonington, was destroyed in a 1938 hurricane.

The Old Lighthouse, Stonington, Conn.

c. 1940s, Westerly News Co., Westerly, RI [$6-8]

Stonington Light, now the Old Lighthouse Museum, Stonington. Erected in 1841 to replace an older light tower, and made obsolete in 1889 by the Stonington West Breakwater Light.

c. 1950s, B. L. Gordon Photo [$7-8]

Stonington Lighthouse, replaced an older light in 1841.

Stratford Point Light House, Stratford, Conn.

pre-1920, H.H. Jackson, Bridgeport, CT [$6-8]

Stratford Point Lighthouse, Stratford.

c. 1960s, NATCO, Douglaston, NY [$4-6]

Delaware

CAPE HENLOPEN LIGHTHOUSE, REHOBOTH BEACH, DEL.

c. 1910s, The Mayrose Co., Linden, NJ [$6-10]

Cape Henlopen Lighthouse, Rehobeth Beach.

31—Replica of Henlopen Lighthouse at Night, Rehoboth Beach, Del.

REPLICA
Henlopen Lighthouse
Built 1725
Rebuilt by Merchants
of Philadelphia
and Delaware
1764
Destroyed by Storms
April 13, 1926

c. 1940s, Harry P. Cann & Bro. Co., Baltimore, MD [$5-7]

Cape Henlopen Lighthouse. A replica still draws tourists, but the original lighthouse was built in 1725, and rebuilt in 1764. Built one mile inland, an eroding shoreline finally claimed the original during an April storm in 1926.

Delaware Breakwater Lighthouse, Lewes. Also known as the East End Light. Construction began in 1828, with completion about six years later.

c. 1990s, Kevin N. Moore/© Marketplace Merchandising, Lewes, DE [$4-6]

Fenwick Island Lighthouse

c. 1970s, Tingle Printing Co., Pittsville, MD [$4-6]

Fenwick Island Lighthouse

1956, Tingle Printing Co., Pittsville, MD [$6-8]

Fenwick Island Lighthouse. Built in 1857, it stands 80 feet high on the site of the Transpeninsular Survey Line, which heads west to the Mason-Dixon line.

FOURTEEN FOOT BANK LIGHTHOUSE

Fourteen Foot Bank Lighthouse. One in a series of seven lighthouses that lined the shoreline of the Delaware Bay, located in the lower part of the Bay, on the western side of the shipping channel. First lit in 1886, it has been automated since 1972.

Florida

Cape Florida Light, Near Miami, Fla.

Greetings from Key Biscayne

Cape Florida Lighthouse, Key Biscayne. Built in 1825, this lighthouse has had a difficult history. It was destroyed by fire during an Indian attack in 1836, and rebuilt 10 years later to its present height of 95 feet. It was then abandoned in 1878 and fell to ruin for many years. Now restored and painted white, it is a proud landmark in a state park.

25

P-5—Charter Fishing Fleet and Hillsboro Light Hillsboro Inlet, Pompano Beach, Fla.

1946, C. T. Art-Colortone/ F.E.C. News Co., West Palm Beach [$5-7]

Hillsboro Inlet Lighthouse, Pompano Beach. First lit in 1907 and automated in 1974, this iron structure towers 137 feet.

1967, Scenic Vendors/ Dukane Press, Hallandale, FL [$4-6]

Jupiter Inlet Light, Palm Beach. Established in 1860 and automated in 1987, the light marks the Loxahatchee and Indian River junction. The 105-foot brick tower was built on a foundation of oyster shells.

c. 1990s, Martin Gordash Photo/ © Scenic Florida Distributors [$4-6]

Key West Lighthouse. Built in 1846, this 86-foot brick tower stands in the midst of a bustling tourist city. Deactivated in 1969, it was recently restored and is now a museum

1973, Florida Natural Color, Inc. [$4-6]

Mosquito Inlet
Light House
on the Halifax River,
near Daytona, Fla.

c. 1910s, E. C. Kropp Co., Milwaukee [$6-8]

The Beauty of Daytona Beach,
"The Lighthouse"

c. 1945, Daytona Beach News Service, Inc. [$5-7]

Mosquito Inlet Lighthouse. First lit in 1887, it was automated in 1953 and is a current aid to navigation. The conical brick tower stands 175-feet high.

Sanibel Island Light, Point Ybel. Established in 1884, the light was automated in 1949.

St. Augustine Light, Anastasia Island. The oldest city in the country, St. Augustine built a watchtower on Anastasia Island to guard the city from pirate attacks. In 1824 a lens was installed in the old watchtower and St. Augustine became Florida's first lighthouse. The original tower was replaced with the 165-foot tower shown in 1874.

Georgia

c. 1930s, E. C. Kropp Co., Milwaukee [$6-8]

St. Simons Island Lighthouse. Built in 1808, it was destroyed during the Civil War and rebuilt in 1871. It is now home to the Museum of Coastal History.

c. 1970s, Caroll Burke Photo/ Dixie News Co., Savannah, GA [$5-7]

Tybee Island Lighthouse, Savannah. Established in 1736, a storm damaged the tower in 1741. A year later a new lighthouse was constructed, and another in 1773. The third stood 100 feet high, but was damaged in the Civil War. The current lighthouse, built in 1869, was rebuilt to a height of 154 feet.

Hawaii

Kilauea Lighthouse. Built in 1913 at the northernmost point of the island state, the light, inactive since 1976, was the landfall light for ships arriving from the Orient.

Diamond Head Lighthouse, Honolulu, built on the steep coast cliff of the extinct Diamond Head Volcano. Built in 1917, this 55-foot tower of reinforced concrete stands 147 feet above sea level and projects its light 18 miles out into the Pacific Ocean.

Illinois

c. 1990s, © Phil Valdez Photo/Illinois Distributing Co., Aurora [$4-6]

Chicago Lighthouse, Chicago Harbor.

Maine

1914, Geo. W. Quimby [$7-9]

The Bailey Light House, Cobbosee Lake.

Bass Harbor Head Light, Mt. Desert Island

Bass Harbor Light, Mt. Desert Island. Located within Acadia National Park and operated by the Coast Guard, the light marks the entrance to Blue Hill Bay.

01801 Mt. Desert Island, Me. Bear Island Light.

pre-1920, T. A. McIntire, Seal Harbor, ME [$12-15]

Bear Island Light -- Northeast Harbor, Maine

c. 1970s, Paul A. Knaut, Jr. Photo/ Bromley & Co., Inc., Boston, MA [$4-6]

Bear Island Light, Mt. Desert Island. Located at the mouth of one of the busiest harbors along Mt. Desert Island, leading into Northeast Harbor.

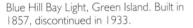

Blue Hill Bay Light, Green Island. Built in 1857, discontinued in 1933.

1973, Augustus D. Phillips & Son, Northeast Harbor, ME [$5-7]

c. 1960s, Wakefield Trading Co., Wakefield, MA [$4-6]

1969, Bugbee Brown, Inc., Biddeford, ME [$4-6]

Boon Island Light. The tallest light in Maine at 137 feet on a dot of land 9 miles off shore, where stranded sailors of the Nottingham Galley were reported to have resorted to cannibalism in 1710. First built in 1780, it was rebuilt in 1805 and 1811, the light was manned until the Blizzard of 1978 when two light keepers saw their quarters, the supply building, and the boathouse completely blown off the island. They took shelter in the lantern room until a Coast Guard helicopter rescued them a day or two later. A large solar panel supplies power to the light today.

Burnt Island Light. Built 1821, this 30-foot stone tower is the innermost light in Boothbay Harbor.

SOUTH PORTLAND, ME. BREAKWATER LIGHT, FORT GEORGES IN THE DISTANCE.

BREAKWATER LIGHT, ROCKLAND, ME.

Breakwater Light, Rockland. Fort Georges is pictured in the distance, beyond a sailing vessel at anchor.

VINAL HAVEN, ME. BROWNS HEAD LIGHT

c. 1915, Hugh C. Leighton Co., Portland, ME [$7-9]

Browns Head Light,
Vinal Haven.

1965, Eastern Illustrating, Belfast, ME [$4-6]

c. 1970s, Don Sieburg Photo/ Colourpicture Publishers, Inc., Boston, MA [$4-6]

Cape Neddick Light, York Beach. This light is also
known as Nubble after its barren, rocky island home.
The 41-foot tower was first established in 1879,
constructed of cast iron plates lined with brick. The
fourth-order Fresnel lens flashes red every six seconds,
and is visible for 13 miles.

Cuckold's Light. Guards the outer
entrance to Boothbay Harbor.

c.1970s, Rudy's Wholesale Distributors, Inc., Meredith, NH [$4-6]

Cape Elizabeth, Me.,
Two Lights.

66469

1916 [$5-7]

CAPE ELIZABETH LIGHT *Maine*

c.1990s, © Tom Mitchell Photo/ Maine Scene Inc., Union, ME [$4-6]

Cape Elizabeth Light

c.1990s, © d Elvidge Photo/ Coastal Exposures, Inc., Southwest Harbor, ME [$3-5]

TWO LIGHTS MAINE

Cape Elizabeth Lights. First called Two Lights when built in 1829 roughly 300 yards apart. The east tower beacon is now automated and the most powerful on the New England Coast – its 4 million candlepower flashing white light is visible for 27 miles. The western tower was decommissioned in 1924.

c. 1990s, © Paul Star Photo/ Maine Scene Inc., Union, ME [$3-5]

Curtis Island Light, Camden, Maine

92950-N

Curtis Island Light, Camden.

c. 1920s, Genuine Curteich, Chicago [$5-7]

LIGHTHOUSE AT COBBOSSEECONTEE LAKE, MANCHESTER, MAINE.   72986

Ladies Delight Lighthouse, Lake Cobbosseecontee. Built on the lake in 1905, this is said to be Maine's only freshwater lighthouse.

1925, CT Co., Chicago [$5-7]

Crabtree Ledge Light, Frenchman Bay, Me.

Crabtree Ledge Light. Northerly part of Frenchman Bay and about one quarter mile off the easterly shore of Crabtree Neck.

c. 1915, Hugh C. Leighton Co., Portland, ME [$7-9]

Dyce's Head Light, Castine.

c. 1970s, Eastern Illustrating Co., New London, NH [$4-6]

Eagle Island Light

c.1990s, © ourtney Thompson Photo, www.Mainescene.com [$4-6]

Eagle Island Light, between North Haven and Deer Isle. Built in 1839.

EAGLE ISLAND LIGHT NEAR NORTH HAVEN, ME.

c. 1910, Hugh C. Leighton Co., Portland, ME [$8-10]

c. 1940s, Sherman's Book and Stationery, Bar Harbor, ME

Egg Rock Light, Frenchman Bay, Me.

c. 1915, Hugh C. Leighton Co., Portland, ME [$5-7]

Egg Rock Light, built in 1875 on a small island to mark the entrance to Frenchman's Bay.

Ferry Landing Light, Islesboro.

c. 1960s, Eastern Illustrating & Publishing Co., Inc., Belfast, ME [$5-7]

Fort Point Light. On the southeasterly side of Old Fort Point and the westerly side of the mouth of Penobscot River.

1910, Robbins Bros. Co., Boston [$8-10]

Franklin Island Light in Muscongus Bay, on the southeasterly side of an entrance to the St. George River.

c. 1915, Hugh C. Leighton Co., Portland, ME [$8-10]

Goat Island Light, a 25-foot brick tower first established in 1822, rebuilt in 1859. Now automated.

c. 1960s, Eastern Illustrating Co., Tenants Harbor, ME [$4-6]

pre-1920, G.W. Morris, Portland, ME [$10-12]

Goose Rock Light, Vinalhaven.

c. 1960s, Luther S. Phillips, Bangor, ME [$7-8]

Great Duck Island Light on the southern point of the island faces the unbroken expanse of the North Atlantic. The westernmost hills of Mount Desert appear on the distant horizon.

1911, Hugh C. Leighton Co., Portland, ME [$12-14]

1938, W. H. Boardman, Dark Harbor, ME [$10-12]

Grindle Point Light, Islesboro.

Halfway Rock Light, midway between Cape Small Point and Cape Elizabeth, built in 1871.

Indian Island Light, Rockland.

Isle Au Haut Light, built in 1907. Now a private bed and breakfast in Acadia National Park.

Libby Island Light, Machias.

Lobster Point Light, Marginal Way, Ogunquit.

Mulholland Point Lighthouse, Lubec, on Campobello Island.

Marshall Point Light House, Port Clyde, Me.
Published in Germany for G. W. Morris, Portland, Maine.

Marshall Point Light, built in 1832 in Port Clyde.

CAMDEN, ME. NEGRO ISLAND LIGHT

Negro Island Light, Camden.

Monhegan Light, Monhegan, Me

Monhegan Island Light. Built in 1824 in the center of the island, 178 feet above the waterline.

c. 1960s, Colourpicture Publishers, Inc., Boston [$4-6]

Owl's Head Light, Rockland, Maine

1946, Genuine Curteich, Chicago [$4-6]

OWL'S HEAD LIGHT, ROCKLAND, MAINE.

c. 1930s, Tichnor Quality Views [$6-8]

Owl's Head Light, built in 1826. Though only 26 feet high, it casts light 16 miles out to sea. A long series of steps leads up to the rocky headland, now a Coast Guard residence located in a picturesque state park. Many ships have wrecked here, and legend includes a tragic tale of "frozen lovers" whose ship wrecked on the point during a blizzard in 1850.

Permaquid Light. Established in 1827 to mark the extreme tip of the peninsula.

c. 1960s, Bromley & Company, Inc., Boston [$4-6]

PETIT MANAN LIGHT
MAINE

c.1990s, © Peter Ralston Photo/ Maine Scene, Inc., Union, ME [$4-6]

Petit Manan Light. On a small island 2.5 miles off Petit Manan Point, this light was first established in 1817 and rebuilt in 1855.

Pumpkin Island Light, Little Deer Island.

1910, Hugh C. Leighton Co., Portland, ME [$7-9]

Ram Island Light, Boothbay.

1933, Hugh C. Leighton Co, Portland, ME [$7-9]

Sequin and Pond Island Lights. One of the oldest lights on the east coast, the Seguine Light, left, was first built in 1795, and later rebuilt in 1820 and 1857. It is the state's highest light at 186 feet above the water. On the other side of the mouth of the Kennebec River sits Pond Island Light, built in 1821 and rebuilt in 1855.

c. 1990s, Commodore Cards, Ocean Park, ME [$4-6]

1975, Owen Art-Color, Newcastle, ME [$4-6]

Portland Head Light Station. One of four colonial lighthouses authorized by George Washington, this is the original building dedicated by General Lafayette. First lighted in 1791, it stands 101 feet above sea level and the beacon is visible up to 30 miles offshore.

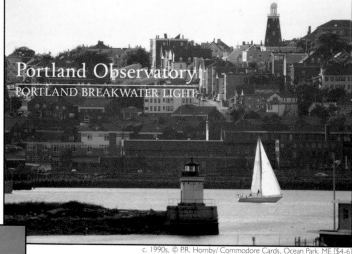

c. 1990s, © P.R. Hornby/ Commodore Cards, Ocean Park, ME [$4-6]

Portland Observatory Light and Portland Breakwater Light. Built in 1875, these two lights overlook Fort Gorges and the Casco Bay. The breakwater light was designed to resemble a fourth-century Greek monument.

c. 1990s, © P.R. Hornby/ Commodore Cards, Ocean Park, ME [$4-6]

LIGHTHOUSE, PROSPECT HARBOR, ME. S.W.

c. 1940s, Eastern Illustrating & Publishing, Belfast, ME [$15-20]

Prospect Harbor Light. Built in 1850, the light marks the east side of the harbor entrance. It was deactivated between 1859 and 1870. The granite lighthouse attached to the keeper's house was replaced in 1891 by the present 38-foot wood lighthouse and a new 1 1/2 story farmhouse-style keeper's house. The lantern held a fifth order Fresnel lens, was automated in 1934, and in 1951 was replaced by an automatic modern optic.

Pumpkin Island Light

c.1990s, Coastal Colour Products, Scarborough, ME [$4-6]

Pumpkin Island Light. Located on a small, rocky islet. Built in 1854, it was discontinued in 1935 and is now privately owned.

c.1960s, Eastern Illustrating, Tenants Harbor, ME [$4-6]

West Quoddy Light. Thomas Jefferson signed the order in 1806 authorizing its construction. The tower was finished in 1808 and rebuilt in 1858. The light guided ships through the Quoddy Narrows, between the U.S. and Canada. It is located on the most easterly point of land in the United States. Also a Coast Guard station.

c.1960s, Guy E. Nicholas Photo/ A Mike Roberts Color Production, Berkeley 2, CA [$4-6]

East Quoddy Head Light, New Brunswick. On the northern point of Campobello Island, the light is a guide to Passamaquoddy Bay between Maine and New Brunswick, Canada.

Ram Island Light. Built in 1877 and rebuilt in 1905, the light marks the north side of the Portland Harbor entrance. It was converted from kerosene to electric in 1958.

Rockland Breakwater Light. Built in 1888, rebuilt in 1902, the light and keeper's quarters were built at the end of a mile-long breakwater guarding Rockland Harbor.

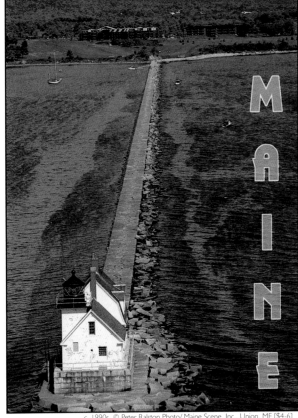

Saddleback Ledge, Penobscot Bay, Me.

Saddleback Ledge,
Penobscot Bay.

Spring Point Light, Portland Harbor. Built in 1897, the brick tower on iron caisson "spark plug" light had a fifth-order lens. Originally 300 yards offshore, it is now at the end of a breakwater built in 1950.

Whitlocks Mill Light. Near Calais, on the St. Croix River, the light shines across the border to Canada.

Wood Island Light. Though the 71-foot tower built in 1808 still stands off the Maine coast from Biddeford Pool, the keeper's quarters have drastically altered since this image was rendered.

Maryland

Concord Point Lighthouse, Havre de Grace. The oldest continuously operated lighthouse in the States, the 32-foot structure has been in operation since 1827. It is situated where the Susquehanna River empties into the Chesapeake.

c. 1990s, Karl Walet Photo, Savannah, GA [$6-8]

Cove Point Lighthouse. This 51-foot tower has marked the Patuxent River entrance since 1828. It was automated in 1986, and the well-preserved site is managed by the Calvert County Marine Museum.

North East, MD

C. 1990s, Traub Co., Baltimore, MD [$4-6]

Gilber Lighthouse Pavilion, North East. This functional lighthouse doubles as a community picnic spot.

c. 1990s, Karl Walet Photo, Savannah, GA [$6-8]

Craig Hill Light. Marking Sparrows Point in the Chesapeake Bay, Baltimore County. First lit in 1873, the Front Range, shown, has two lights, one at 22 feet, one at 39 feet, and is located 2.4 miles south of the rear range. Automated in 1964.

Chesapeake Bay Maritime Museum, St. Michaels

c. 1990s, Traub Co., Baltimore, MD [$4-6]

Hooper Straight Lighthouse, St. Michaels. One of the three remaining screwpile lighthouses in the Chesapeake Bay. The existing 41-foot tower was first lit in 1879 in Tangier Sound. It was deactivated in 1966 and moved to its Chesapeake Bay Maritime Museum setting the following year.

Piney Point Lighthouse, Potomac River. The oldest of eleven lighthouses originally built in the Potomac River and one of only four remaining. The 35-foot white conical tower is 14 miles upstream, built in 1836 and active until 1964.

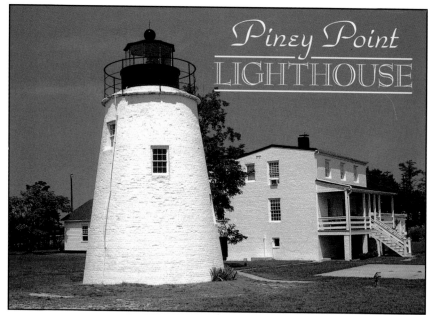

c. 1990s, D. Traub Co., Baltimore, MD [$4-6]

Poole's Island Lighthouse, Aberdeen. Built in 1825, the 40-foot conical tower was operational until 1939.

c. 1990s, John Houck Photo. [$7-8]

Sandy Point Shoal Lighthouse, upper Chesapeake Bay at the Bay Bridge. Built in 1883, this functioning tower was automated in 1963.

c. 1990s, Karl Walet Photo, Savannah, GA [$7-8]

c. 1990s, Karl Walet Photo, Savannah, GA [$4-6]

Seven-Foot Knoll Lighthouse, relocated from the Patapsco River in the Chesapeake Bay to Baltimore's Inner Harbor in 1987. First lit in 1855, it is the oldest surviving screwpile light on the Chesapeake Bay.

c. 1970s, Scenic Views Photography/ Dynacolor Graphics, Inc., Miami [$5-7]

Thomas Point Light, Annapolis. The last screwpile structure left on its original site in the bay, it went into service on November 27, 1875, to replace a light on the Thomas Point shore at the entrance to the South River. With its red roof and white sides, this picturesque lighthouse is a fine example of its type. The light and fog signal, both now automated, are still active.

Turkey Point Lighthouse

Turkey Point Lighthouse, at the confluence of the North East and Elk Rivers overlooking the Chesapeake Bay. Built in 1833, the 35-foot tower sits atop a 100-foot bluff, making it the highest of seventy-four lighthouses on the bay. Originally equipped with a Lewis Lamp, which used an Argand-style lamp and a reflector, it was changed to a Fresnel Lens which used a lamp that burned spermaceti (whale oil), switched to kerosene in late 1870s, incandescent oil vapor lamp in late 1800s, and electrified in 1943.

c. 1990s, © Mark M. Wachsman Photo [$5-7]

c. 1960s, Wakefield Trading Co., Wakefield, MA [$4-6]

pre-1920, Hugh C. Leighton, Co., Portland, ME [$5-7]

Annisquam Lighthouse. Established in 1801 on Wigwam Point, overlooking Ipswich Bay.

c. 1900s [$6-8]

Boston Light. First lit in 1783. The 89-foot tower was built of rubble stone on a granite ledge on Little Brewster Island in Boston Harbor. Originally lit by tallow candles, the present lens was installed in 1859 and automated in 1998.

c. 1900, New England News Co., Boston [$5-7]

Bug Light, Boston Harbor.

c. 1970, J. Lazarus, Hyannis, MA [$4-6]

Brant Point Lighthouse, Nantucket. Built in 1746, the original wooden tower burned in 1758, the next blew down in 1774, and then it burned again in 1774. The standing 26-foot brick tower was built in 1856.

Butler's Flat Lighthouse, New Bedford off Clark's Point. Built 1898, this 53-foot cylindrical brick tower incorporates the three-story keeper's quarters. It is an unusual design, with the sparkplug tower built of brick rather than cast iron. The original fifth order Fresnel lens is still in use.

c. 1945, New Bedford News Co., New Bedford, MA [$4-6]

Chatham Light, Cape Cod

DEER ISLAND LIGHT BOSTON HARBOR MASS

Chatham Light, Cape Cod. Established in 1808, this lighthouse and lifeguard station are situated on a high bluff overlooking the Atlantic. One of the most powerful lights on the coast.

Deer Island Light, Boston Harbor. Established at the entrance to Boston's Inner Harbor off the southern end of Dear Island in 1890, it was demolished in 1982.

Copyright 1906 by the Rotograph Co.

G 7155 Eastern Point Light House, Cape Ann, Mass.

The Lighthouse Eastern Point, East Gloucester, Mass.

Eastern Point Light, Gloucester, MA. Established 1832, it is still active, and the two-story Victorian keeper's quarters (1879) are used as Coast Guard housing.

Graves Light, Massachusetts Bay. Established in 1905, the name is enticing, though the ledges actually were named for Thomas Graves, who was a Vice Admiral of the Navy in the 1600s. Nonetheless, there have been many shipwrecks in the area, including the sinking of the City of Salisbury in 1938, when more than $1 million in cargo was lost. The keeper's house actually comprised three of the five stories within the lighthouse itself.

c. 1915 [$5-7]

c. 1960s, Mayflower Sales Co., Provincetown, MA [$4-6]

c. 1970s, National Park Service Photo/ Colourpicture, Boston, MA [$4-6]

Highland Light, Cape Code. The oldest light in Cape Cod, originally built in 1797 and reconstructed in 1857, it is also the highest and most important light on Cape Cod. Automated since 1986, it is still a functioning U.S. Coast Guard Light. Locally known as Highland Light, on maritime charts it is officially named Cape Cod Light. In the mid-1990s, erosion of the shoreline caused Highland Light to be moved back from the edge of the cliffs.

Hospital Point Light, Beverly. Built in 1927.

Minot's Ledge Light. One of many lights in the Massachusetts Bay, situated at the entrance of Boston Harbor between Scituate and Nantasket Beach. Famous for its highly exposed location, the first tower (1850) was swept away by waves in less than a year (April 1851). This tower took five years to build and is still considered a major engineering accomplishment. It was restored in 1989.

Marblehead, on Lighthouse Point at the northern tip of Marblehead Neck. Established 1835, it is a 105-foot square pyramidal tower with a central cylinder. The keeper's quarters were demolished in the 1960s.

Nauset Light, Cape Cod. This 89-foot wooden tower was built in 1875, originally the north tower at Chatham, which at the time had twin towers. In 1923 it was moved to Eastham, near Nauset Beach and became Nauset Light. Threatened by coastal erosion, it was moved back a safe distance in 1996, followed a few years later by the keeper's house.

Nobska Point Light, Woods Hole. Guarding the approach to Woods Hole Harbor for steamers and ferries sailing to Martha's Vineyard and Nantucket since 1876.

Race Point Lighthouse, Provincetown. Established in 1816, the current lighthouse was built in 1876 on the extreme tip of Cape Cod.

Sankaty Light, Siasconset, Nantucket Island. This 70-foot brick and granite tower was built in 1849, the first U. S. lighthouse equipped with a Fresnel lens as its original optic. It is now critically endangered by erosion of the cliff it occupies, and fundraising to move the light is underway.

SANKATY LIGHT, SIASCONSET, NANTUCKET ISLAND, MASS. BUILT 1850   3978-29

c. 1990s, Peter Meggison Photo, Modern Postcard [$4-6]

Tarpaulin Cove Lighthouse, Naushon Island, MA. Established in 1817, the current tower was built in 1856 on the largest of the Elizabeth Islands, between Buzzard's Bay and Vineyard Sound.

c. 1970s, © J. Lazarus, Hyannis, MA [$4-6]

West Chop Light House, Martha's Vineyard. Built in 1817, the stone tower had to be moved back from the eroding bluff in 1838. In 1846 a new tower was built of rubble masonry, and in 1892 the rubble tower was replaced with the current brick tower.

1972, Howell Studio Photo/Colourpicture, Boston, MA [$4-6]

West Chop Light House, Vineyard Haven

c. 1970s, Yankee Bazaar, Edgartown, MA [$4-6]

Wood End Light
PROVINCETOWN

Wings Neck Light, Bourne. Built in 1849 to protect heavy marine traffic in Buzzards Bay traveling to ports in Wareham and Sandwich. Damaged by fire, it was rebuilt in 1889. When the Cape Cod Canal opened in 1914, Wings Neck became one of the most important lighthouses on the Atlantic Coast. By 1943, it had become obsolete. The property was sold by the government in 1947 and is now privately owned.

Wood End Lighthouse, Provincetown. Built in 1872 between Race Point and Long Point, and directly across from Provincetown Harbor.

Michigan

Michigan has 3,100 miles of shoreline bordering on four of the five Great Lakes. Over 100 lighthouses dot its coasts, more than any other state.

Au Sable Point Lighthouse, Grand Marais, Lake Superior. Established in 1958, this conical brick structure has been automated since 1958, when the original third order Fresnel lens was replaced by a 300 mm solar-powered beacon.

Bete Grise Lighthouse, Mendota. Established in 1870 to mark the Mendota ship channel from Keweenaw Bay to Lac La Belle, it was decommissioned in 1960, then reactivated in 1998.

Bete Grise

BIG BAY POINT LIGHTHOUSE

Big Bay Point Lighthouse, Lake Superior, Big Bay. Established in 1896 and automated in 1945, this still-active navigation beacon is privately owned and one of only two lighthouses in Michigan that operates as a bed and breakfast inn. (The other light is Sand Hills Lighthouse.)

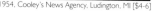

Big Sable Point Lighthouse

1954, Cooley's News Agency, Ludington, MI [$4-6]

LIGHTHOUSE AT BIG POINT SAUBLE, LUDINGTON, MICHIGAN

c.1990sMarvin Aerial Photography/ Perrin Souvenir Distributors, Northville, MI [$4-6]

Big Sable Point Lighthouse, Ludington, Lake Michigan. One of the few Michigan lighthouses with a tower topping 100 feet, it was built in 1867 to a height of 112-feet. In 1902, the deteriorating brick tower was encased in steel.

Charlevoix South Pier Lighthouse. Marking the channel entrance from Lake Michigan to the city of Charlevoix. The first pier light of 1885 was a square wooden structure located on the north pier and was moved to the south pier in 1914, then was replaced by the current light. The current light is anchored on a small, square tower at the end of a concrete pier. It is about 100 feet from shore.

Charity Island Lighthouse
MICHIGAN

c. 1990s, Marvin Aerial Photography/ Perrin Souvenir Distributors, Northville, MI [$4-6]

Charity Island Lighthouse, Big Charity Island, MI. The light stands on a barrier island between Lake Huron and Saginaw Bay. It was active from 1857-1939.

Charlevoix

c.1990s, John Penrod Photo/ Penrod/Hiawatha® Co., Berrien Center, MI [$4-6]

Cheboygan Crib Light. Established in 1852 as a crib light outside the Cheboygan Harbor, it was relocated to a display point in the harbor.

Copper Harbor Lighthouse. Established in 1866 to mark the tip of the Keweenaw Peninsula along the rugged Lake Superior shoreline. It was deactivated in 1933.

Crisp Point Lighthouse, Paradise, Lake Superior. Once a thriving light station, the site has been deactivated since 1947, and now marks a lonely stretch of beach 18 miles off the main road.

Detroit River (Bar Point Shoal) Lighthouse, Lake Erie. Located in the lake, just south of the entrance to the Detroit River, this station has been active since 1875.

c.1990s, Marvin Aerial Photography/ Perrin Souvenir Distributors, Northville, MI [$4-6]

Eagle Harbor Lighthouse, Lake Superior. Built in 1871 to replace an 1851 structure, the beacon broadcasts from the harbor entrance at Keweenaw Peninsula.

c.1960s, W.R. Kristo Photo/ The Office Shop, Calument, MI [$4-6]

Fort Gratiot Lighthouse, Lake Huron. Marking the point where the St. Clair River and Lake Huron meet at Port Huron, this 86-foot tower has been lit since 1929.

c.1990s, Carl J. Perrin Photo/ Perrin Souvenir Distributors, Grand Rapids, MI [$4-6]

c. 1970s, James Blank Photo/ Perrin Souvenir Distributors, Northville, MI [$5-6]

c.1970s, Raymond J. Malace Photo/ Perrin Souvenir Distributors, Grand Rapids, MI [$4-6]

Grand Haven Lighthouses. Several lights guide brisk light traffic in one of Michigan's most picturesque harbor towns. The first historic tower (inner light) was first lit in 1905. It is a red conical cast iron tower standing 51 feet high.

c.1990s, John Penrod Photo/ Penrod/Hiawatha® Co., Berrien Center, MI [$4-6]

Grand Marais Harbor Range Lights, Lake Superior. Shown is the second Historic Tower, the rear or inner range light, first lit in 1908.

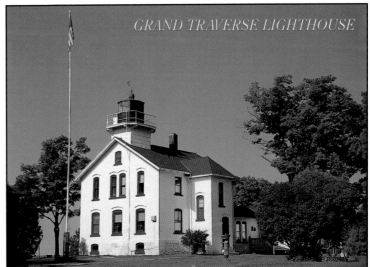

c.1990s, John Penrod Photo/ Penrod/Hiawatha® Co., Berrien Center, MI [$4-6]

Grand Traverse Lighthouse Leelanau Peninsula, Lake Michigan. Established in 1852, this light was automated and deactivated in the same year – 1972. It's now a museum.

Granite Island Light, Lake Superior. Crafted from rough coursed granite blocks in 1868, the light tower is 10 feet square and 40 feet high. One of the oldest surviving lighthouses on the lake, it became less important to navigation in the 1920s when shipping ran less often between the island and shore, and is now inactive.

c. 1990s, Marvin Aerial Photography/ Perrin Souvenir Distributors, Grand Rapids, MI [$4-6]

Gratiot Light, St. Clair River.

1905 [$7-9]

Gull Rock Lighthouse, between Copper Harbor and Manitou Island. True to its name, the light has stood over a large population of gulls, along with many loons, since 1867.

c.1990s, John Penrod Photo/ Penrod/Hiawatha® Co., Berrien Center, MI [$4-6]

Hazensisle, Houghton
Lake Heights.

Harbor Beach Light, north side
breakwater entrance to Lake Huron.
Established in 1858 and still active.

Huron City Light House on the shores of Lake Huron, near Port Austin and Caseville in the
Michigan Thumb District.

Holland Harbor Light, south pier of Holland. Known as "Big
Red" to local fishermen and mariners along Lake Michigan's
eastern shore, it has been a landmark since 1936.

Little Cape Sable Lighthouse near Silver Lake and Michigan's famous Dunes.

c. 1960s, Penrod Studio, Berrien Center, MI [$5-6]

© 1967 Hiawatha Card Co., Mackinaw City, MI/ Lucy Gridley Photo [$5-6]

Mackinaw Lighthouse provided navigational aid along the Straits of Mackinac from 1872 to 1957.

Munising Lighthouse, Munising.

c. 1960s, Hiawatha Card Co., Ypsilanti, MI [$5-6]

Old Presque Isle Lighthouse on Lake Huron, 23 miles north of Alpena, MI, was built in 1840.

1979, A. Dean Watkins Co., Lansing, MI [$4-6]

5575—Palmer Park Lighthouse, Detroit, Mich.

1909 [$5-6]

Log Cabin and Lighthouse, Palmer Park, Detroit, Mich.

1916 [$5-7]

Palmer Park Lighthouse, Detroit, with a replica of the log cabin in which Senator Thomas W. Palmer resided.

c. 1960s, Upper Michigan Card Co., Manistique, MI [$4-6]

Pointe Aux Barques Lighthouse, Huron City. Built in 1857.

c. 1950s, Mirro-Krome ® Card by H.S. Crocker Co., Inc., San Francisco [$5-6]

Point Betsie Lighthouse and Coast Guard Station near Frankfort.

c. 1950s, Acro Distributing, Evanston, IL [$5-6]

Port Austin Lighthouse marks a rocky shoal at the tip of the Michigan Thumb, about 2.5 miles north of Port Austin Harbor.

c. 1960s, Kramer News Co., Port Huron, MI [$5-6]

Port Huron Lighthouse on Lake Huron.

Port Sanilac Lighthouse, Lake Huron.

Presque Isle Lighthouse on Lake Huron near Rogers City.

Round Island Lighthouse, built in 1894 to help ships pass from the St. Mary's River to Lake Michigan through the passage between Round Island and Mackinac Island.

Seul Choix Pointe Lighthouse, built in 1892, stands 80 feet tall and can be seen from a radius of 17 miles.

107-D   Split Rock Lighthouse, 200 Feet Above Beautiful Lake Superior

c. 1940s, St. Marie's, Gopher News Co., Minneapolis, MN [$5-6]

Split Rock Lighthouse commands one of two cliffs a quarter of a mile apart on Lake Superior.

c.1970s, Penrod/Hiawatha Card Co., Berrien Center, MI [$5-7]

South Manitou Light, first established in 1839 at 35 feet tall, a total of 65 feet above lake level, proved inadequate. It was reconstructed in 1872 to 104 feet tall, with the new lens focal plane at 130 feet above lake level. The light was decommissioned in 1958.

c. 1950s, L. L. Cook Co., [$5-6]

Tawas Point Lighthouse near East Tawas.

WHITE RIVER LIGHTHOUSE

White River Lighthouse at the cities of Whitehall and Montague.

White Shoal Light

White Shoal Light in Northern Lake Michigan is one of two lights that mark the Gray Reef Passage between Beaver Island and Waugoshance Point.

Minnesota

123-D   Lighthouse, Entrance Duluth-Superior Harbor, Duluth, Minn.

Duluth-Superior Harbor Lighthouse, Duluth, marking the narrow canal entrance to the harbor from Lake Superior.

73

Two Harbors
Lighthouse

Two Harbors Lighthouse, 1892, sits on the shore of Agate Bay along Lake Superior's North Shore.

Slip Rock Lighthouse on the North Shore Drive of Lake Superior.

Biloxi Lighthouse, built in 1848, is a 65-foot tower overlooking the Gulf of Mexico.

Victorian Lighthouse, built in the late 1800s by a wealthy family to help guide their four racing sloops to safety. Now owned by the city and operated as a tourist attraction.

Mark Twain Memorial Lighthouse, on Cardiff Hill, Hannibal, Missouri

PHOTO BY B. E. EMERSON

1950, Hannibal News Co. [$5-6]

Mark Twain Memorial Lighthouse provides a magnificent view of steamboats on the Mississippi.

Pla-Port Lighthouse, Lake of the Ozarks, Missouri

c. 1940s, Corwin News Agency, Jefferson City, MO [$5-6]

Pla-Port Lighthouse is the only privately operated lighthouse on any inland lake in the United States. The Lake of the Ozarks is 130 miles long.

New Hampshire

FORT CONSTITUTION AND FORT POINT LIGHT, NEW CASTLE, N. H.

c. 1920s, C.T. American Art [$5-7]

FORT POINT LIGHT, NEWCASTLE, N. H.   185-29

1929, C. T. American Art Colored [$5-7]

c. 1970s, Ft. William and Mary Committee, N.H. [$4-6]

1970, Carleton Allen Photo/ Eastern Illustrating Co., New London, NH [$4-6]

Fort Point Light at Fort Constitution, Newcastle. The lighthouse station was established in 1771, and in 1791, the State of New Hampshire gave the United States the neck of land on which Fort William and Mary and a lighthouse were situated, a peninsula on the northeast corner of New Castle Island overlooking both the Pisquatua River and the Atlantic Ocean. The fort was repaired and renamed. The present, 48-foot tower cast-iron lighthouse was built in 1877 and automated in 1960.

c. 1970s, Eastern Illustrating Co., New London, NH [$4-6]

c. 1960s, Don Sieburg Photo/ Colourpicture Publishers, Inc., Boston [$4-6]

WHITE ISLAND LIGHT, ISLES OF SHOALS, N. H.
6030. COPYRIGHT, 1901, BY DETROIT PHOTOGRAPHIC CO.

©1901 Detroit Photographic Co. [$7-9]

Isles of Shoals Light, White Island. Established in 1821, it is located 5.5 miles off the coast, the light towers 82 feet and can be seen for 15 miles at sea. Automated in 1986.

Newfound Lake Light, Bridgewater.

The Lighthouse and Ledges, Newfound Lake, Bristol, N. H.   Hand Colored

1941, Frank W. Swallow Post Card Co. Inc., Exeter, N.H. [$7-9]

Loon Island Lighthouse, Lake Sunapee, N. H.

Loon Island Light, Lake Sunapee. Established 1893, with a new lighthouse built in 1960.

1B627-N

c. 1920s, C. T. American Art [$5-7]

Whaleback Light. Built in 1872 of granite blocks with the keeper's quarters integrated into the tower, it is owned and operated by the town of Kittery, Maine. The light was positioned to protect the Portsmouth, NH, harbor. Today the light shines a revolving DCB-224 airport-style beacon.

WHALEBACK LIGHT, PORTSMOUTH, N. H.

6334. COPYRIGHT, 1902, BY DETROIT PHOTOGRAPHIC CO.

©1902 Detroit Photographic Co. [$7-9]

WHALEBACK LIGHT

c. 1990, © P.R. Hornby/ Commodore Cards, Ocean Park, ME [$4-6]

Absecon Lighthouse, Atlantic City, N. J.

© 1906 [$6-8]

Barnegat Light, N. J.

1971, Parlin Color Co., Inc. [$5-6]

Barnegat Lighthouse. Built in 1857-58 by the Federal Lighthouse Board to replace the earlier, 1834 light. First lit January 1, 1859, it rises 165 feet above sea level. Now on the National Register of Historic Places.

THE FAMOUS BARNEGAT LIGHT

Absecon Light. Card is inscribed, "This is to help light your collection."

1941, Art Photo Greeting Co., Elizabeth, NJ [$7-8]

3519—Lighthouse. Atlantic City, N J.

c. 1910 [$6-8]

Ship John Shoal Lighthouse. Named after the Ship John, which wrecked nearby in 1787. The iron superstructure was part of the 1876 International Centennial Exhibition in Philadelphia before being placed in the Delaware Bay near the mouth of the Cohansey River in 1877. Still working.

© 2000 "The Lighthouse Lady"/ Carole F. Reily Photo [$4-6]

Brandywine Shoal Lighthouse. This light station at the southernmost part of the Delaware Bay went into operation in 1850 and was the last lighthouse in the bay to have a keeper on board. Automated in 1974.

Cape May Point Lighthouse.

East Point Lighthouse. Last remaining beacon in a series of seven lighthouses that lined the shoreline of the Delaware Bay. Built 1849 and commissioned in 1852. Still working.

© 2002 Wyco Colour, Merion Station, PA/ Carole F. Reily Photo [$4-6]

Elbow of Cross Ledge Lighthouse-
Delaware Bay,
Off of Fortescue, N.J.

Elbow of Cross Ledge Lighthouse. Once one in a series of seven lighthouses that lined the shoreline of the Delaware Bay, first lit in 1910. The light's four-man crew slept in life jackets in expectation of the repeated blows they received from passing ships. Now an automated steel tower atop the original base near Fortescue, NJ.

© 2002 Wyco Colour, Merion Station, PA/ Carole Reily Photo [$5-6]

Hereford Inlet Lighthouse. Built 1872 and first lit 1874 with a fixed white beam that radiated 14 miles out to sea. Now a beacon for tourists.

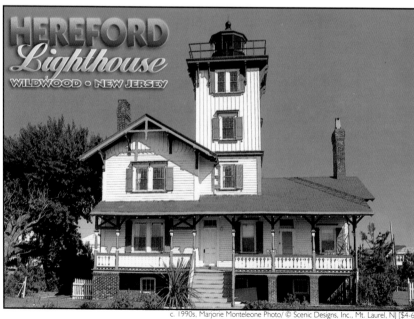

c. 1990s, Marjorie Monteleone Photo/ © Scenic Designs, Inc., Mt. Laurel, NJ [$4-6]

Ledge Lighthouse,
Delaware Bay,
off Fortescue, N. J.

Ledge Lighthouse. Once one in a series of seven lighthouses that lined the shoreline of the Delaware Bay. First lit in 1875, it was replaced by the Elbow Cross Ledge Light and discontinued around 1907. The deteriorated structure was burned down to the stone base in 1962.

Miah Maull Shoal Lighthouse. Once one in a series of seven lighthouses that lined the shoreline of the Delaware Bay, it was named after a man who drowned near the present site. The fourth order Fresnel lens replaced a temporary light in 1913, and was automated in 1973.

MIAH MAULL SHOAL
LIGHTHOUSE - Delaware Bay,
S.E. of Fortescue, N.J.

Navesink Twin Lights. The first site of America for many who crossed the Atlantic, these two lights were built in 1862 at the highest point on the state's Atlantic coast to mark the entrance to the New York Harbor. Now a state museum.

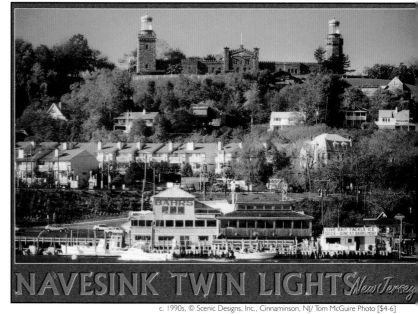

SANDY HOOK LIGHTHOUSE, N.J.

Sandy Hook Lighthouse. The fifth lighthouse built in the United States in 1764 and the oldest still operating, it stands 90 feet tall and has eight equal sides.

Barcelona Lighthouse, 1828, in Chautauqua County. Claims to be the first and only lighthouse in the world lit by natural gas.

1956, Mc Clenathan Printery, Inc., Dunkirk, NY [$4-6]

Bug Lighthouse marks the entrance to Orient Harbor and the waters of the East End.

LONG ISLAND

BUG LIGHTHOUSE

© 1999 East End Greetings, Cutchogue, NY [$4-6]

BUFFALO, N.Y.
China Lighthouse

China Lighthouse protects the entrance to the Buffalo River at Lake Erie.

c.1990s, James Blank Photo/ © S.H.E.L. Ad Products, Gr. Isl., NY [$4-6]

c. 1910, H.C. Leighton Co., Portland, ME [$6-7]

Dunkirk Lighthouse at Point Gratiot was constructed in 1875 and is still an active aid to navigation. The 61-foot tower still has its original third order Fresnel lens, with a 17-mile range that makes it one of the most prominent on Lake Erie.

c. 1940s, Art Photo Greeting Co., Elizabeth, NJ [$7-9]

Eaton's Neck Lighthouse, 1798, on the east side of Huntington Bay entrance has a fixed white light and third order Fresnel.

c. 1960s, Milt Price Photo/ Tomlin Art Co., Northport, NY [$4-6]

Execution Rocks Lighthouse, 1850, midway between Manhasset and Hempstead Bays on Long Island Sound.

1953, Louis Dormand, Riverhead, NY [$4-6]

c. 1908 [$6-8]

Fire Island Lighthouse, 1858, is the first to be sighted by ships arriving from Europe.

1909, Souvenir Post Card Co., New York [$6-8]

Charlotte-Genesee Lighthouse. The original lighthouse built to mark the west bank of the Genesee River as it emptied into Lake Ontario was built in the early 1800s and now sits inland from the lake, a historic site as pictured in the more recent post card. The other light shown was the "new west pier light" from 1884 to 1931, and has subsequently been replaced twice by different structures.

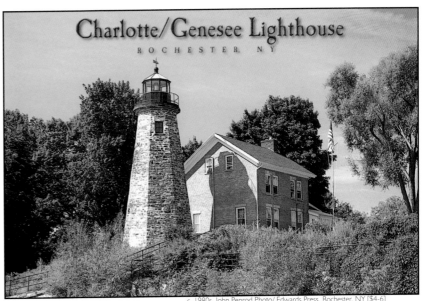

c. 1980s, John Penrod Photo/ Edwards Press, Rochester, NY [$4-6]

Seneca Lake Lighthouse, Geneva.

1917 [$5-7]

Horton Point Lighthouse, a 58-foot tower built in 1857 on the Long Island Sound.

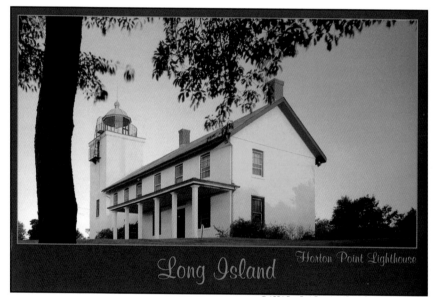

© 1996 East End Greetings/ Ralph Pugliese Photo [$4-6]

Hudson River Lighthouse sits in the center of the river, between Athens and Hudson City. The beacon was established in 1874 to guide mariners away from a shallow mud shoal.

c. 1915, Ruben Publishing Co., Newburgh, NY [$5-6]

The Hudson River

Tarrytown Lighthouse, built in 1883, was the southernmost in series of eight lighthouses that provided navigational aid to ships on the Hudson River and guarded river traffic from dangerous shoal water on the river's eastern shore.

HUNTINGTON HARBOR LIGHTHOUSE

Huntington Harbor Lighthouse marks the entrance of Lloyd Harbor and Huntington Harbor. The 42-foot tower was built in 1912, automated in 1949.

Latimer Reef Lighthouse in Fishers Island Sound, between the mainland of Connecticut and Fishers Island.

Little Gull Island Lighthouse, 1868, is located seven miles northeast of Orient Point between the Long Island and Block Island Sounds.

LONG ISLAND

Little Gull Island Lighthouse

c. 1950s, Milt Price Photo/ Tomlin Art Co., Northport, NY [$5-6]

Montauk Point Lighthouse has marked the extreme tip of Long Island since its completion in 1796.

1955, Dave Edwardes Photo/ Tomlin Art Co., Northport, NY [$5-6]

Orient Point Lighthouse guides vessels in Long Island. It was constructed in 1899 to mark the end of Oyster Point Reef on the western side of Plum Gut.

c. 1950sLouis Dormand Photo/ Dormand Postcard, Riverhead, NY [$5-6]

Outer Light House, Fair Haven, N.Y.

Outer Lighthouse, Fair Haven.

c. 1920, Illustrated Postal Card, New York [$7-9]

Race Rock Lighthouse, 1878, southwest of Fisher's Island in Long Island Sound.

Greetings From Fishers Island

c. 1955, © Sedge LeBlang Photographers, Carnegie Hall, NY [$4-6]

c. 1910, Miller Paper Co., Inc. Syracuse [$5-7]

Rock Island Light, 1847, one of several lighthouses throughout the 1000 islands region, located near Fishers Landing along the St. Lawrence River.

1949, Wm. Jubb Co., Inc. Syracuse, NY [$5-6]

Rondout II Lighthouse, Kingston, marks the mouth of Rondout Creek on the Hudson River. Built in 1913, it is now a museum.

c. 1990s, Bill Herman Photo/ Pendor Natural Color, Pearl River, NY [$4-6]

c. 1970s, Holdt Studio, Pulaski, NY [$4-6]

Selkirk Light, Pulaski, 1838, marks the mouth of the Salmon River on Lake Ontario.

Sunken Rock Light, Bush Island, protects ocean-bound vessels in the 1000 Islands section of the St. Lawrence River.

Tarrytown Lighthouse on the Hudson River.

c. 1915, Chas. W. Hughes, Mechanicville, NY [$5-6]

Stony Point Lighthouse, Hudson River.

c.1960s, Gray's Wholesale, Clayton, NY [$4-6]

1917, the American News Co., NY [$5-6]

c. 1950s, Marks & Fuller, Inc., Rochester, NY [$5-6]

Tibbets Light, Cape Vincent, which marks the outlet of Lake Ontario, was fist built in 1827, and rebuilt in 1854.

c. 1960s, Sterling Wholesale Co., Gouverneur, NY [$5-6]

West Point Lighthouse on the Hudson River.

View down Hudson River, from the Bend at West Point.

c. 1905, The American News Co., NY [$5-7]

Baldhead Lighthouse - Smith Island, N.C.

Photo: Jim Doane

© 1974 Aerial Photography Services, Charlotte, NC [$5-6]

Baldhead Lighthouse, Smith Island, was built to guide marine craft up the Cape Fear River and past the feared naked bleak elbow of sand that juts far into the ocean from lower Cape Fear.

c. 1970s, Hugh Morton Photo/ Elizabeth City News, NC [$5-6]

Bodie Island Lighthouse, Outer Banks. Established in 1848, the 170-foot brick tower is attached to a brick oil house. The original first order Fresnel lens is still in use. The original two-story brick duplex keeper's quarters is a visitor's center (museum and gift shop). Two outbuildings have also been preserved.

1957, Sides Photos, Nags Head, NC [$5-6]

Cape Hatteras. Shown prior to a recent move inland, this light was first put to use in 1870 to warn ships off the dangerous, storm-lashed shallows of Diamond Shoals. At 193 feet, it is the tallest brick lighthouse in America, and now a museum in Cape Hatteras Seashore National Park.

c. 1950s, Elizabeth City News Co., NC [$4-6]

c.1970s, Bob Glander Photo/ Elizabeth City News Co., NC [$4-6]

Cape Lookout Lighthouse, South Core Banks. Built in 1859, this 163-foot brick tower is painted in a black-and-white diamond pattern unique in the U.S.

Currituck Lighthouse, Corolla, NC. Built in 1875, this red brick lighthouse still guides mariners to safety.

Oak Island, Caswell Beach. Built in 1958, the 155-foot cylindrical reinforced concrete tower is the second tallest concrete light tower in the country. The three colors – the black of the upper third, the central white area, and gray bottom – were created in concrete, not painted. It marks the west side of the entrance to the Cape Fear River.

Ocracoke Lighthouse, Ocracoke Island. Built in 1823, this is the second oldest beacon in use on the Atlantic coast.

Ashtabula

c. 1990s, © Jim Doane Photo, Victory Postcards [$4-6]

Ashtabula Lighthouse was moved to its current location in 1916. It stands 40 feet above Lake Erie. During a fierce ice storm in 1928, two keepers were imprisoned and had to thaw the door and tunnel through ice five feet thick in order to escape.

Cleveland West Pierhead

c. 1990s, © Jim Doane Photo, Victory Postcards [$4-6]

Cleveland West Pierhead Lighthouse was built at the end of a four-mile concrete pier in 1911 to guide ships to the entrance of Cleveland Harbor and the Cuyahoga River.

Fairport Harbor West Breakwater

Fairport Harbor West Breakwater in Fairport was established in 1825. Because of structural damage, it was abandoned shortly after the Civil War.

Lighthouse, Northwood, Mercer County, Celina, Ohio

Grand Lake Lighthouse, also known as the Northwood Lighthouse, is a reproduction of England's famed Eddystone Lighthouse at Land's End.

Lorain Lighthouse, built in 1917, has been inactive for nearly 30 years. The original fourth order Fresnel lens was removed in 1965.

c. 1980s, James R. Spring Photo/ Newspper Sales Inc., Cleveland, OH [$4-6]

1926, Alexander Mfg. Co., Sandusky, OH [$5-6]

Marblehead Light near Lakeside, Ohio, is the oldest ship beacon on the Great Lakes. Construction began in 1819 on the 50-foot tower, built of native limestone five feet thick at the base and narrowing to two-foot thick walls at the top.

1963, D. S. Kirkpatrick, Lakeside, OH [$4-6]

PORT CLINTON, ON LAKE ERIE

c. 1990s, William E. Gordon Photo/ Nu-Vista Prints, Willowick, OH [$4-6]

Port Clinton Lighthouse once guarded the entrance to the Portage River, and now marks the entrance to Brands Marina.

South Bass Island Lighthouse

South Bass Island Lighthouse, built in the 1890s on the south side of the island north of Port Clinton, OH.

c.1990s, John Penrod Photo/ Penrod/Hiawatha, Berrien Center, MI [$4-6]

Toledo Harbor Lighthouse

Toledo Harbor Lighthouse, built in 1904 eight miles from shore in Lake Erie.

c. 1990s, © Richard Newman Photo/ Victory Postcards [$4-6]

Turtle Island
Lighthouse Ruins

Turtle Island Lighthouse, now in ruins following its 1831-1904 years of service, after which it was replaced by the Toledo Harbor Light.

c. 1990s, © Richard Newman Photo/ Victory Postcards [$4-6]

A replica of the 1877 Vermilion Lighthouse was built in 1992 for the grounds of the inland Seas Maritime Museum.

Inland Seas
Maritime Museum

c. 1990s, Nu-Vista Prints, Willowick, OH [$4-6]

Oregon

Cape Arago Light near Coos Bay was built in 1934 to replace two earlier structures dating back to 1866. The tower is 44 feet tall, rising 100 feet above the water.

c. 1950s, Smith-Western Co., Inc., Tacoma, WA [$5-6]

965—CAPE BLANCO LIGHT HOUSE, MOST WESTERN POINT ON COAST, OREGON COAST HIGHWAY

PHOTO BY SAWYER   2A184

1942, Wesley Andrews Co., Portland, OR [$5-7]

Cape Blanco Lighthouse towers above the western-most point in Oregon, 9 miles north of Port Orford. The oldest standing lighthouse on the Oregon Coast, it was commissioned in 1870.

c. 1970s, Columbia View Cards, Ocean Park, WA [$4-6]

Cape Mears Lighthouse, Tillamook.

Coquille River Lighthouse
at Bandon by the Sea.

Heceta Head Lighthouse

c. 1950s, Anderson Scenic Post Cards, Portland, OR [$4-6]

Heceta Head Lighthouse

COLOR BY MORTON LUMAN

1970, Smith-Western Inc., Portland, OR [$4-6]

Heceta Head Lighthouse, commissioned in 1894, warns ships from the rocky shoreline just north of Florence.

Built in 1997, this is the second and newest privately owned lighthouse on the West Coast, located on a bluff in the picturesque Port of Brookings.

c. 2000, © Steven Astillero/ Nature's Design Photography, Medford, OR [$4-6]

1953, Wesley Andrews Co., Portland, OR [$5-6]

Tillamook Head Lighthouse between Seaside and Cannon Beach.

c. 1980, Mel Anderson Photo/ J & H Sales, Portland [$4-6]

948 UMPQUA LIGHT HOUSE, OREGON COAST HIGHWAY

PHOTO BY WESLEY ANDREWS

7A-H3958

c. 1940s, Wesley Andrews Co., Portland, OR [$5-6]

c. 1970s, John McNamara Photo/ Columbia View Cards, Ocean Park, WA [$4-6]

Umpqua River Lighthouse in Winchester Bay was built in 1894. The 65-foot tower is one of the few lights along the Pacific Coast that emits both white and red alternating flashes.

989 YAQUINA LIGHT HOUSE, YAQUINA HEAD

PHOTO BY WESLEY ANDREWS

OREGON COAST HIGHWAY

1946, Wesley Andrews Co., Portland [$5-6]

283. CAPE FOULWEATHER, "THE LIGHTHOUSE BY THE SEA", AT NEWPORT, ORE., THE FAMOUS TOURIST RESORT.

1915, Lipschuetz Co., Portland, OR [$5-7]

c. 1990s, © Steven Astillero Photo/ Nature's Design Photography, Central Point, OR [$4-6]

Yaquina Lighthouse, Oregon's tallest and second oldest lighthouse was built in 1873. It stands on the forebodingly named Cape Foulweather in Newport.

54 *Light House and Inlet to Erie Bay, Erie, Pa.*

Erie Bay Lighthouse at the inlet to Erie Harbor.

c. 1940s, C. T. Art Colortone [$6-8]

Presque Isle Lighthouse, built in 1872, is the second lighthouse built on Lake Erie.

©1999 Gold Star Photography/ Photo © 1999 Bernik, Erie, PA [$4-6]

108

c. 1990s, © B. L. Gordon Photo/ Book & Tackle Shop, Watch Hill, RI [$4-5]

1910, The Rhode Island News Co., Providence [$6-8]

Beaver Tail Light in Beavertail State Park is America's third lighthouse, and the first in Rhode Island, dating from 1749. The original tower burned a few years later and was replaced with a stone tower in 1753. The current square granite tower was built in 1856.

Bristol Ferry
Lighthouse, Bristol.

1907, The Rhode Island News Co., Providence [$6-8]

Castle Hill Lighthouse,
Newport.

c. 1970s, Herbert Pollak Photo/ New England Products, Inc., East Greenwich, RI [$4-6]

Hog Island Shoal Light,
Narragansett Bay.

1913, Hugh C. Leighton Co., Portland, ME [$7-8]

c. 1920s, Hugh C. Leighton Co., Portland, ME [$7-8]

Ida Lewis Lighthouse, Newport. Lime Island Lighthouse was renamed in 1924 after the nationally celebrated daughter of the official keeper. She tended the light for her father and was reported to have saved no less than 18 lives by herself.

1909, A. C. Bosselman & Co., NY [$7-8]

Pomham Lighthouse, Narragansett Bay.

c. 1960s, Stanley J. Szelka Photo/ LK Color Productions, Providence, RI [$6-7]

Point Judith Lighthouse, Narragansett. Point Judith Light and Coast Guard Station sit on the western entrance to the Narragansett Bay. The first wooden tower was built in 1810, but was blown over during a storm six years later. A replacement stone tower lasted until 1857, when the current octagonal tower was erected.

1969, LK Color Production, Providence, RI

Pomham Light, Providence. Located on the east side of Providence River, the station was established in 1871. The 40-foot wood tower is still standing today, along with its oil house, though service was discontinued in 1974.

1906, S. Langsdorf & Co., NY [$7-8]

c. 1990s, © Bernard Ludwig Gordon Photo/ Book & Tackle Shop, Westerly, RI [$5-6]

1906, A. Negus, Block Island, RI [$7-8]

Southeast Light, Block Island. Established in 1875, the massive Victorian brick structure was moved 245 feet inland from the edge of Mohegan Bluffs in 1993.

Warwick Light Station overlooks Narragansett Bay in Warwick Neck. The 55-foot tower was built in 1827 and was moved 75 feet inland in 1938.

View from Watch Hill House, Watch Hill, R. I.

Watch Hill Light. Built in 1808 and replaced in 1856 with the current granite block tower. Its fourth order Fresnel lens is still active.

HARBOUR TOWN MARINA

Hilton Head Island. This cast iron tower was first lit in 1880 and served until 1932. Later it was moved to its present location in the Harbour Town Marina.

c. 1990s, © . Cornelia Photo/ SouthArt, Inc., Hilton Head Island, S.C. [$4-6]

Hunting Island Lighthouse. Established in 1859 and built in 1873, this 136-foot tower had to be moved in 1889 to escape erosion. The interior was renovated in 1991, and it is now open to the public.

c. 1990s, © Martha Lawrence Photo/ SouthArt, Inc., Hilton Head Island [$4-6]

MORRIS ISLAND LIGHTHOUSE

c. 1990s, © Ricky Riggs Photo/ Charleston Post Card Co, Inc., Charleston, SC [$4-6]

Morris Island Lighthouse. This 150-foot lighthouse was first built in 1876 some 1,200 feet from the ocean. It's now located "off" the east end of Folly Beach and fundraising is underway to preserve it.

"Silent Sentinel"

Bolivar Lighthouse

c. 1990s, © Stephen Myers Photos/Island Shots, Galveston, TX [$4-6]

Point Bolivar Lighthouse. Standing on the Bolivar Peninsula it shone across the shipping lanes from Galveston Island from 1872 to 1933.

Port Isabel Lighthouse. Built in 1853, it was deactivated only twelve years later and is now a state historic site.

PORT ISABEL LIGHTHOUSE   TEXAS

c. 1990s, © Richard Stockton Photo/ Coastal Cards, Port Isabel, TX [$4-6]

Vermont

c. 1970s, Forward's Color Productions, Inc., Manchester, VT [$4-6]

Colchester Reef Lighthouse. Established in 1871 and deactivated in 1933. Once a beacon on Lake Champlain, this wooden, Second-Empire style structure was relocated inland to the Shelburne Museum.

Virginia

Assateague Light, Chincoteague National Wildlife Refuge. Built in 1866-67, the 145-foot brick tower stands guard over the treacherous shoals that lie off the barrier islands. The original lens was a first order Fresnel. The light was automated in 1965.

c. 1970s, F.W. Brueckmann Photo/ Tingle Printing Co, Pittsville, MD [$7-8]

533:—Old and New Lighthouse, Cape Henry, near Norfolk, Va.

c. 1930s, Asheville Post Card Co., Asheville, NC [$6-8]

61:-OLD LIGHTHOUSE AT CAPE HENRY, VA.

1910 [$6-8]

Old and New Cape Henry Lighthouses, Virginia Beach. The Old Cape Henry Lighthouse was built in 1791, the first erected by the U.S. Government. The newer lighthouse, built in 1881, is the tallest cast iron lighthouse in the country, operated by the U.S. Coast Guard. Its signal, visible 19 miles at sea, beckons sailors to the entrance of the Chesapeake Bay.

New Lighthouse, Cape Henry, near Norfolk, Va.

1947, Frank G. Ennis Paper Co., Norfolk, VA [$6-8]

OLD POINT COMFORT LIGHTHOUSE
FORT MONROE, VIRGINIA

c. 1990s, © on & Linda Card Photo/ Cards Unlimited Inc., Keysville, VA [$4-6]

Old Point Comfort Lighthouse, Fort Monroe. Constructed by the Federal government in 1802, the light has been in continuous use ever since. Automated in 1973, the structure is operated by the U.S. Coast Guard.

Washington

Beacon Lighthouse, Grays Harbor.

CAPE
DISAPPOINTMENT
LIGHTHOUSE

c. 1970s, Photo'Neil, Long Beach WA [$5-6]

c. 1970s, Photo'Neil, Long Beach WA [$4-6]

Cape Disappointment Lighthouse overlooks all river traffic crossing the Columbia River Bar with 58,000 candlepower.

1975, Ellis Post Card Co., Arlington, WA [$4-6]

Fort Casey Lighthouse overlooking Admiralty Inlet and guarding the entrance of Puget Sound.

c. 1970s, Columbia View Cards, Ocean Park, WA [$4-6]

Grays Harbor Light, built in 1898 at Point Chehalis, the tower is 107 feet high and has 180,000 candlepower.

547—NORTH HEAD LIGHT HOUSE ILLUMINATING COAST OF WASHINGTON

Ilwaco's North Head Lighthouse marks the Long Beach Peninsula for ships trying to gain access to the Columbia River. Built in 1898, the 64-foot tower stands 194 feet above sea level.

Lime-Kiln Lighthouse, San Juan Island.

Point No Point Lighthouse, built in 1879 overlooking Puget Sound near Hansville.

Point Wilson Lighthouse at the northeast tip of the Olympic Peninsula, which juts into Admiralty Inlet separating Puget Sound from Juan de Fuca Strait.

Algoma Lighthouse, 1893, is considered one of the most photographed beacons in the Midwest. Still active, it commands a pier in Lake Michigan.

c. 1990s, Jim Leuenberger Photo/ © Scofield Souvenir & Postcard Co. [$4-6]

Bailey's Harbor Upper and Lower Rangelights align to aid sailors entering the harbor.

c. 1990s, Steve Gibson Photo/ © Scofield, Inc. Menomonee Falls, WI [$4-6]

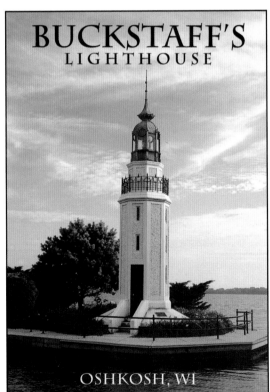

c. 1990s, Darryl R. Beers Photo/ DC Distributions, Sister Bay, WI [$4-6]

Buckstaff's Lighthouse on Lake Winnebago, once known as Bray's Point Lighthouse, was built around 1911 to guide boats past dangerous reefs at the mouth of the lower Fox River.

c. 1940s, Oshkosh News Co., Oshkosh, WI [$6-7]

Cana Island Lighthouse Door County

c.1990s, Jim Leuenberger Photo, © Scofield Souvenir & Postcard Co, Menomonee Falls, WI [$4-6]

Cana Island Lighthouse in Door County north of Bailey's Harbor.

DOOR COUNTY
Chambers Island Lighthouse

Chambers Island Lighthouse built in 1868 to serve the west shipping canal from the port of Green Bay.

c.1990s, Photo by Darryl R. Beers, DC Distributions, Sister Bay, WI [$4-6]

DOOR COUNTY
Eagle Bluff Lighthouse

c. 1990s, Darryl R. Beers Photo, DC Distributions, Sister Bay, WI [$4-6]

Eagle Bluff Lighthouse was built in 1868 to guide mariners through the east shipping lane of Strawberry Channel.

c. 1960s, Wyman Post Card Co., Wausau, WI, [$5-6]

Light House at the Harbor Entrance, Green Bay, Wis. — D-4

c. 1940s, P & J Distributing Co., Green Bay, WI [$5-6]

The Lighthouse at South Entrance to Lake Park, Milwaukee.

1913, E. C. Kropp Co., Milwaukee [$7-8]

Lake Park Lighthouse, Milwaukee.

Green Bay Lighthouse marks the west side of the entrance to the dredge channel leading into Green Bay Harbor. The circular house is 25 feet in diameter, with the upper floor divided into rooms for the keepers.

Lakeside Park Lighthouse at Fond du Lac on Lake Winnebago.

c. 1950s, L. L. Cook Co., Milwaukee, WI [$4-6]

© 1960, L. L. Cook Co. [$4-6]

Milwaukee Breakwater Light at the entrance to the Port of Milwaukee.

Outer Island Lighthouse, established in 1873, is one of six light stations in the Apostle Islands.

Pilot Island Lighthouse at the tip of the Door County Peninsula was built in 1851.

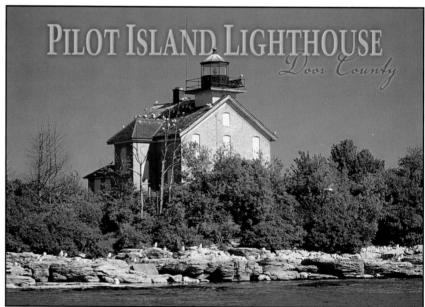

Plum Island Lighthouse, built in 1897 in Door County.

Potawatomi Lighthouse, Rock Island, was the first lighthouse built in Wisconsin, first in 1836, with a replacement in 1858.

Port Washington Light at the harbor entrance.

Racine Reef Lighthouse, located 3 miles from shore in 1908. The structure was destroyed in the 1960s, and replaced with a skeletal tower.

Sherwood Point Lighthouse, Door County.

127

STURGEON BAY

CANAL STATION

c. 1980s, Moonlight Photography, DC Distributions, Sister Bay, WI [$4-6]

Sturgeon Bay Lighthouse
in Door County.

1830   WIND POINT LIGHTHOUSE, RACINE, WISCONSIN

5A-H2664

1943, E. A. Bishop, Racine, WI [$7-8]

c. 1950s, L.L. Cook Co. [$5-6]

Wind Point Lighthouse, built in 1880,
towers 112 feet above Lake Michigan.